I am grateful to God for everything! And I believe that the meaning of life is to make sense of other lives. C.A., you are the meaning of my life.
Lov U

ROBERTO MEIRELLES
2024

This Book Belongs to:

Test Color Page

Doctor Strange

hulk

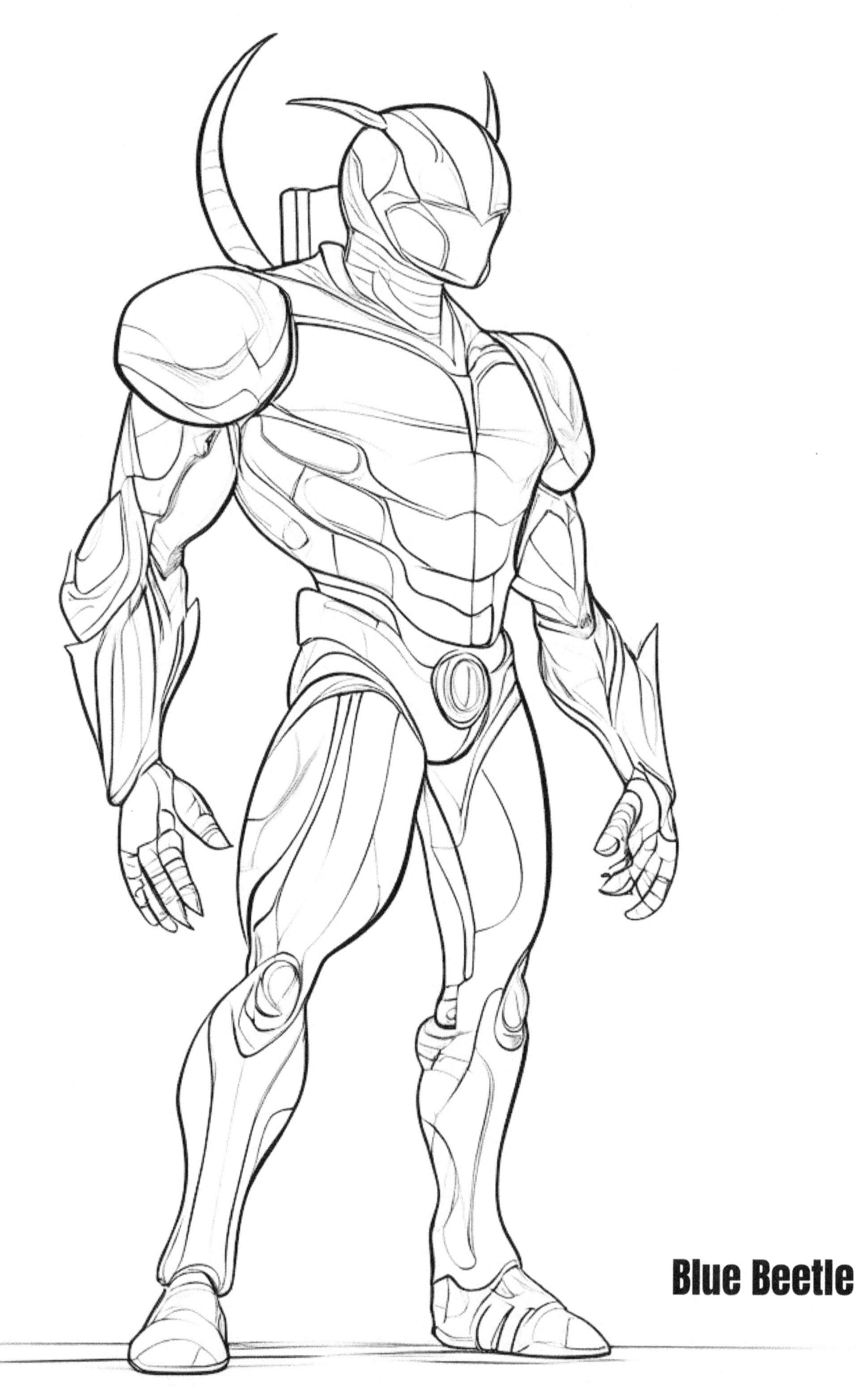

Blue Beetle

Cybord

Deadpool

Flash

Joker

Wolverine

Captain Atom

Demolisher

Iron man

Wonder
Woman

Superman

Ant Man

captain
America

Spider man

Ghost_Rider

THOR

Batman

Scarlet
Witch

Black
Widow